PRAYERS FOR PEOPLE LIKE ME

To my dear friend

I feel we have been
on the high road
together.

You know my love
and

God's
all the way

Bob St Clair
July 14,
1989

PRAYERS FOR PEOPLE LIKE ME

Robert James St. Clair

BIBAL Press
Berkeley, California

Cover design by: Abigail Johnston

Library of Congress Cataloging-in-Publication Data
St. Clair, Robert James, 1925-
    Prayers for People Like Me / Robert James St. Clair
      p. cm.
    1. Prayers. I. Title.
BV245.S64 1989   89-7206
242'.8051--dc20   CIP
ISBN 0-941037-09-6

Copyright © 1989 by Robert James St. Clair
Published by BIBAL Press, Berkeley, CA 94701
Printed by GRT Book Printing, Oakland, CA 94601

This book is dedicated to

My Aunt Bess

Elizabeth Stanecker

July 11, 1896 to July 11, 1988

A Mighty Prayer Warrior

Whose love and prayer have surrounded me

from the day of my birth

and follow me still

ACKNOWLEDGEMENTS

I would like to acknowledge my unpayable debt of thanksgiving for a Bible-centered Church and its staff—The First Presbyterian Church of Berkeley, California—for enthusiastic requests for these prayers, where they were first lifted to God. You will get a prayer meeting in this Church at the drop of a hat.

I want to thank one of its families, that of Gary and Carolyn Yee, for their penetrating discussions and insistence that these prayers be published.

I especially thank Pastor Earl Palmer for his ongoing and delightful vision of this book of prayer. More than once he has stopped in the middle of a worship service, turned to me, thanked me, and then proceeded to discuss the morning prayer.

I am grateful to Joanne Dills, my faithful booster and critic, who has carefully read everything I've written. She is a model and inspiration for prayer.

Last, but hardly least, I wish you could feel the passion and dedication of the publisher, Duane Christensen, and of my editor, Joycelyn Moulton, who have turned hard work into an adventure in enrichment.

CONTENTS

HE PRAYS FOR THE PEOPLE

Robert St. Clair is a good friend and a fellow pastor in ministry. We have known each other for some ten years and he has been a parish associate in our congregation. This non-paid position has been a very joyous relationship for me and the people. One of the very best parts of the relationship has happened on Sunday mornings in our church, the First Presbyterian Church of Berkeley, when Bob St. Clair shares in our common worship in the time of the Prayer of the People. His prayers have brought the man Bob into my life and along side of my journey; but more than that they have pointed my heart to the Lord of the Church, Jesus Christ. I welcome this book that will make his prayers available to the wider family that this book will now create because there is a timeless and particular relevancy about these prayers for worship.

Though poetry is present in these words of prayer with their economy of language and intensity of feeling, what is more vital is that earnestness and depth of real faith is here too. These prayers come from someone who hurts and struggles and sings and loves and hopes; and since I feel that way too, the prayers in these pages could be borrowed by my own heart and mind as I turn my eyes toward the Jesus who hears our prayers.

I believe this volume will be helpful to those who in their own journey will appreciate the way that a new streak of light breaks in upon new and old issues or problems as this fellow journeyer has prayed from his heart. There will also be those moments of sheer whimsy too with the exciting humor of real life lived before the Lord who told of laughter in heaven for sinners who repent; the joy of these prayers are as impressive to me as the empathy.

Thank you Bob, for bringing this volume together as a gift to people who are learning to pray as we are learning to live in fellowship with God.

Rev. Earl F. Palmer
Berkeley, California

PRAYER: A PARTNERSHIP WITH GOD

In Luke 18:35-41 a persistently studious and deeply spiritual blind man cries Messianic titles at Jesus of Nazareth until the procession stops. He is brought before the Lord, front and center. He slowly reaches out to trace the form of Christ through his robes. He holds his hands on the face of Christ and no one moves. Jesus asks him, "What do you want me to do for you?" The blind man stands there and thinks about the question.

"What do you want me to do for you?" We require God's creative power, God invites us to share our meanings. Together we interpret the world and together we offer light and life.

What do we human beings want? What do we require? To what degree are we in touch with our own situation?

Prayer enlightens us to know what to pray for and fortifies us to take responsibility for what we must face together and none of us can do alone.

It was logical for the blind man to ask for his sight again. He already had demonstrated his dedication to truth and his thirst for light. By a life devoted to prayer and the Scriptures he was able to seize the opportunity for wholeness instantaneously. Apparently he prayed in faith.

The beginning of prayer is demanding. I prefer to focus*
awhile on my whole condition before I say a word. I must
concentrate, reflect, make pictures of life around me, ease into
the drama I am part of, and swim around in the depths. And
all the while I hear the words, "Just exactly what is it you would
like me to do for you?"

Prayer is a working partnership with God in the ongoing
creation of the world. New forms of truth and life are being
created in profusion. Old forms of sin and fear lay like ice on
the life-lines.

Prayer communicates with God in our humanity and in the
name of Christ. Thus, God does not merely understand us. In
prayer God experiences us. In Christ we experience God.

Prayer strikes to the heart of our condition and discloses our
stage of development. At the same time we gauge our condition
through the divine perception.

In prayer we make ourselves available to the Creator's
determination to provide significant fulfillment to persons and
nations. The responsibility which becomes ours is awesome.

"What do you want me to do for you? Prayer is necessary to
God. He wishes to bless life through the Word in flesh and
blood. In prayer our lives become a flower which opens to the
sun. We turn to the light and define ourselves. Prayer thus
enables the Almighty to feel within our feelings, to think within
our thoughts, to transmit meaning to others through our bodies,
to be aware with the utmost sensitivity what our vision is, how
we would like to honor it, and what we most earnestly require
from God if we are to sing: "Bless the Lord . . . and forget not
all his benefits (Psalm 103: 1-2).

---

* *Focusing* by Prof. Eugene Gendlin of the University of Chicago. This book
helps us get in touch with our felt-sense, our total experience at any one point
in time.

In prayer, God's agenda becomes ours. We see the needs of others as our needs also. Whether we are praying for ourselves or for others, the mission of God becomes first and foremost. I mean, here is my Auntie alone in this house, lonesome for her husband of many years who has passed on to glory. "I am praying for you. What do you need?" I hear the words as, "What do you want me to do for you?" I must stop and think, "What is the central thing for me? What is the main issue?" Her prayers lead me to prayer.

I receive new energy, new enlightenment, a new sense of Presence. And the irony of it! Here is this woman alone in a Brooklyn apartment appropriating the mighty power of God for people. I do not know if I feel terrible sadness or sublime joy when the question was posed nightly to her, "And what do you want me to do for you?" and she had only requests for others, and so little for herself.

But I know she had Paul's values in Philippians 4. She was and is satisfied according to God's riches in glory in Christ Jesus.

Prayer warriors are a legacy of the Word made flesh. What can we do but follow them? If prayer is that communication of deepest experience in behalf of creation, then prayer is raised in the idiom of life and life is lived in the quality of prayer.

Robert James St. Clair
Berkeley, California

WHERE ARE YOU

In the market place
  where a restless river
    of humankind
      throbbed on ebb and flow
I stared into each face,
  shifting, my gaze darting
    like frightened fish in the river's swirling,
      circling pools—

From face to face
  I caught a blurred and flashing glimpse
    to see if perhaps
      Christ had slipped
        into our places unknown—

The Lord lost in disguise,
  the mighty light of ages
    now a dark blur, perhaps carried
      like flotsam and jetsam
        on a swollen, heedless river of souls.

Where are you?

    If I stand on this shore
      and cast my voice into the swirling foam—

      Help me!

Will you hear?

If I arrest the next poor soul,
  grasp him in anguish and hold his faith to the sun,
Will it be you?

If I pause to wet the ground with sorrow's endless tears
  and as the sun descends, wait
    and wait
      for some touch to heal this pain,
        Will you be there?

Where are you?
And if at dusk the
  fear and burden of the day
    bring me to an end
      with prayer's final sigh

Can it be that you were in that place
  with my eyes,
    speaking with my voice
      hearing with my ears
        touching through my fingers?
              Would you do that terrible irony, Lord,
                that I was searching
  For you, who had chosen me?

Where are you?

  Lord, are we one?

  Tell me, lest tomorrow
   one searching not find me,
   not find us both—there in his searching heart.

5

PRAYER FOR BEING ALL RIGHT WITH BEING ALONE

Lord God, Creator, who connects every living thing by His Spirit, who gives us power with others through love, significance in our eyes through royal adoption, power over futility through faith, and power over the world through wisdom, bless the tie that binds our hearts to the family of God.

There is a great fear that stalks us, O Lord, called
                    Being Alone.
Young people fear that popular peers will ignore them, and good friends will neglect them.
Parents are certain that children will grow up, leave home, make their own families, and they're probably right.
Years of maturity engenders worry that remaining loved ones will depart and this massive cloud called death will hover over them so that its shadow is depressing and it's never sunny.
Father, we all share the experience of Jesus who agonized in Gethsemane under the shadow of the cross while his comrades slept. Give us the courage to reach out and grasp that state called Being Alone, and make a friend of it.

Challenge us to study the Word, read avidly,
        find people with a good laugh,
            become an expert in something,
memorize the 103rd Psalm, write to a prisoner,
        search out interesting folks,
            study good causes for our money,
learn new recipes, play a tapc for a shut-in,
        drive a very old, old person
            to a significant happening
ask one of the ministers, "If I gave you two hours
        per week, what would you do with it?"
and then dress up for an elegant supper,
        just ourselves, alone.

Alone, yes, but not always completely alone. Never alone while Jesus is there as a friend who sticketh closer than a brother, chatting over old times and new, pointing out the vast world which is His and therefore ours, never alone while He's in touch with loads of ideas and all kinds of people.

Alone? Yes, as we are all alone, even with family and friends flocking around us, and only *we* know the experience of our hearts, our regrets and how little we dare still to hope. Yes, alone, and so Lord God, bless this human nobility of befriending ourselves and becoming a more stimulating person in solitude, who, by your grace, O God, shall always find others to walk with part of the way.

We thank you, O God, for love—and for aloneness—and may their steady engagement grant us an extravagant life without dread. In Christ's name, Amen.

7

SPIRIT

God and Creator of all that exists,
of worlds we see and those beyond us,
of the person our neighbor and those sacred persons
of every nook and cranny of the globe,
we thank you for the glorious messages we receive when
we imagine we are alone or forgotten.
We adore you for the patience of those trying to tell us
"I love you" when we have trouble hearing it.
We thank you for the children
who will not be put off so easily.
We worship you for your Holy Spirit
who has ways of whispering in the night,
of talking again through an old Bible,
of picking the locks when we are bound up in ourselves,
of giving us energy when we are fed up
and slowing us down when we are overheated.
You tune up the symphony in duty, or affection,
of work, or prayer, in the words of someone dear to us,
in the music of hope when we hear,
"Hold on; I will never leave you or forsake you."
As stubborn or indifferent as we seem, O Lord,
your messages have a way of getting through
and in a tough old world we believe in angels.
Thus we have no doubt that
in hours of turmoil or great joy,
when we are just beginning or ending,
at midnight or high noon,
our messages get through to you,
and that when we least remember it, for us,
gracious Lord, life is still prayer.
Through Christ our Lord, Amen.

CELEBRATE DEPENDABLE PEOPLE

Lord God, Creator of Heaven and Earth,
we celebrate the dependable people.
We laugh and sing with those who rebelled
to do their thing,
but we whisper a deep Thank You for the people
who work, rest and work again, day after day.

We share the excitement of liberation,
and we also feel good about the mothers and fathers
who work, raise children, cook meals, clean house
love their careers, and grow mentally and spiritually.
We'd like to hear a blast on the trumpet
for the young people who study, obey the rules,
and pitch in and help others.
While some may consider it rather prosaic,
we have a good word for all those here
who have a calling, whether to write, clean, labor,
type, care, manage, drive, teach, pray, minister,
deliver, consult, study, sell, or be a clerk, and who,
day in and day out, do it for the glory of God,
and for not much besides.
Lord God, three cheers in heaven
for both the prodigal sons and daughters
who returned home at last,
and for their elder brothers and sisters
who, for all their complaints, do their duty,
and keep a home to return to.
We are grateful for the exhilaration of adventure
and the joys of discovery, but
Thank You, God, for those who are there
when we need them.
In the name of Christ Jesus we pray. Amen.

HEALTH AND WELL BEING

To you, O Lord God,
covered by the splendor of light and
alone worthy of our adoration,
we, the people, lift our petitions.
Congratulations Lord,
for your most magnificent creation: the human body.

And Lord have mercy when it starts to fall apart.
Over the years we come to realize that
every faculty we enjoy,
every disease we don't have,
and every miracle we assume will recur
in body and mind
become incredible blessings once they are threatened.
The truth is, our health has been so good
we forget to thank you for it.
So when the stresses and strains of life overtake us,
our Father,
or accident, disease, or a thousand things,
it is then we are startled and ask for explanations.

Actually, we don't need explanations, Lord,
since we remember the good old days,
nothing less than miracles will do.
First and foremost we petition you
for the nearness of Jesus
who helped people care about themselves
as much as He did.

We especially commend to your Son, Christ the Healer,
those ravaged by pain
and fighting for life, at home, and in hospitals.

We ask for the miracle of new sight
to see matters differently,
a new flame in the heart to keep hope burning,
and the miracle of wisdom
to know what to hope for.

We ask for the miracle of ministry,
so that we attend to another's aches and pains
before our own are cured.
We ask for the miracle of a sense of humor,
so that we can regale friends with our symptoms
without boring them to death.
We ask for the miracle of courage and will power
so that we don't accept death
one minute before its time.

And lastly we pray for the miracle of breath and Spirit;
I pray that you, Holy Spirit, will move
gently as a breeze
among us just now.

Breathe into the dust of our being
the breath of life again.
Through Christ our Lord,
Amen.

In the Grip of Winter

Eternal God, Creator of all life, accept our thanksgiving
for the warmth of the sun upon our faces this morning.
Already Springtime whispers to us of coming life
  and new beginnings.
There is the bursting of the power of a thousand suns
  in the unseen tip of your finger.
But some here, O Lord, experience the deadness of
  resentment and the grudges they will not surrender.
Still others are in the grip of a winter of fear,
  dreading the increasing demands of their work,
    the doctor's report,
      their children's letters, and
        the lined face in the mirror.
Still others, O Lord, are gripped by the ice and snow of
  insignificance when others succeed and they don't,
    when families no longer need them,
      when talents are not recognized, and
        dreams now only taunt them.
Over these hearts, still frozen, waft the warm tides
  of a world bathed in fruit and blossoms.
Embrace hearts with excitement in the air,
  planning for work under the sun,
    planting, watering, harvesting.
As we have seen, every storm shall pass at last,
and there is the Lord Jesus Christ,
our ageless friend, deeply in love with us, calling out
  to the fields which were barren and indifferent.
Earth shall surely dance with beauty as our wonder
  at the miracle of life shall never end.
Some here have been waiting too long.
Father, breathe upon the spark of hope within us,
  just now, this moment.
In Jesus' name. Amen

PRAYER WHEN LIFE STAGNATES

What a glorious event this is, O God,
  so worthy of our worship: to be alive and human
  on a magnificent morning in Spring!
It reminds us of Easter and your power
  to take us by surprise.
There are those who, once enraptured by the Good News
  of Christ risen for our sakes,
  now take miracles for granted.
Take them by surprise once more.
There are those of us delighted beyond words
  by new love.
Perhaps a husband and wife need to be surprised
  by how much life has passed them by,
    and how much more is still waiting.
And there are those of us who brag of being survivors,
  as if getting through were the end
    instead of the beginning.
Lord, just when life seems to be getting too stable,
  too predictable, when persons are typed,
    when the Bible is merely studied,
      when precious memories are merely catalogued,
        when the future is relegated to bank accounts,
          and when the children are mainly a chore,
don't stand for it! Break through! Take us by surprise!
Lay down a new challenge
  in a new day with exciting possibilities.
But of course, thank you,
    you will do this anyway.
In the name of Christ our Savior,
  and risen Lord. Amen.

A Prayer to Jesus of Berkeley

On this day of resurrection and life,
of worship and new beginning,
we confess to you, Lord God of heaven and earth,
that the Christ of glory has become an intimate friend,
while the Jesus of Galilee becomes more distant.
We who thank you rightly for warm and lovely homes
regard with despair roving bands of transient men.
We who thank you for daily bread,
honor Christ the Provider,
but when Jesus commanded "feed the poor, feed the poor"
He never seems to be speaking to us.

We adore the Christ, O God, who introduced us
to all these lovely people,
but the Jesus of the city streets
who befriends the friendless,
who touches the leper, and
who embraces the destitute,
does not appear in our circles.
He who said, "Inasmuch as you have done it
to the least of these has done it unto me,"
seems to elude us by His disguises.
We are glad, Lord, for what Jesus of Galilee could do,
but what Jesus of Berkeley is doing
is a secret for some of us.

Keep on forgiving our sin, O Lord, while we hear
again and again,
"Why do you call me Lord—and do *not*
the things which I command you?"

WE PRAISE YOU THROUGH ALL SEASONS

Lord God, we praise the very thought of you
to all of earth and heaven
and we boast of you to all our foes.
We boast of you when life is good,
when love is in its Springtime,
when hopes are bright,
dreams enticing,
trust unbroken,
the Gospel is fresh, and
the children are young.
We boast of you at the first flush of success
and the significance of our burgeoning wisdom.

But then when ice covers the heart,
wisdom turns to cynicism,
the children have taken a strange life,
and we admit some of our dreams
will never be,
then, especially *then*, when they ask us,
"Where is your God?"
then from the mountain tops we shall cry,
"By my side."
Over land and sea, together or alone,
in sickness or in health, we shall boast to all
"Praise God who gives us life,
praise God of the resurrection
and new beginnings,
praise God of love unbroken,
praise God of freedom and might,
praise God from whom all blessings flow,
in this and every age,
in this and every world,"   Hallelujah!

A PRAYER FOR AMERICA

Lord God, under whose sovereign sway
   people and nations live by your permission,
   but not always your blessing,
   throw open wide the throne room door
   to look upon America, for this is our homeland
   and it is a great nation.
Showered by your grace it is a land of perpetual harvest
   and its triumphs are the stuff
   of which dreams are made.
When oppressed people dream of freedom
   they think of us.
And when they think of rule by law and justice
   they think of us.
The one who created Eden walks among us still
   in the cool of the evening,
And we boast more of your magnificent goodness
   than of our prowess when we say, in distant lands,
   "I am an American."
Grant that we shall serve our country loyally,
   by serving the Lord Jesus Christ and His church
   faithfully.
We repent that we have forgotten that
   size is not greatness,
   license is not liberty, and
   token programs for a few poor, a few homeless,
   a few aged, and a few hopeless
   are not worthy of our legacy of
   gracious stewardship from our forbearers.

Like all men arrogant with power, O Lord,
We tend to become bullies toward the weak.
We confess to our shame that in America
    if you're poor you're nobody.
More than cocaine and alcohol we confess our addiction
    to money and power for their own sake.
We are expecting your judgement and our rebirth.
But you have given us hope,
God of our fathers and mothers
Yes, you call on us for leadership.
So call on us for sacrifice and righteous example.
Give our youth uncontainable vitality of faith,
    and a yearning to walk with you
    over the face of the wide world.
We look at the young people who just stepped out of Eden
    with sunlight on their eyes and bouquets in their cheeks.
They look at the world as a rich red apple.
They borrowed our hearts for a song
    and the future never looked so good, O Lord,
    it never looked so good.
May we not fail them
    so that they can boast to their grandchildren,
"Yes, those were dark and troubled times for the world, but
    the light from America never went out."

THANKSGIVING FOR HOPE

Creator of all there is
 GOD silent
            invisible
 GOD only wise, we feel *without words* to describe you
   lacking in moral perception to engage you
      and without the holiness to sense you.

We experience you richly in Christ Jesus
      your son
      our Lord.
He floods our human routine with color and turns it
 into a vigorous and majestic drama.
   Earth is opened to heaven, and
   now, there is much more than we thought
   just beneath the surface
   so much mystery
   so much design and power
      for the life you are creating.
We thank you for the power of hope in Christ.

We thank you in our own lives
      for the joy of hope fulfilled.
We think of the millions of persons without a Savior,
      and we thank you for hope.
We think of the children who will never grow old
      because of poverty or drugs
      and we thank you for hope.
We think of Christ's own land, a cauldron boiling with
      discontent, and we live as He did—in hope.

We think of the dear and precious men and women suffering
    from AIDS or other illness,
        and we thank you for
            medicine
                research
                    friends
                        courage
                            and Easter.
In the darkest nights we thank you
    for pinpoints of light.
You have given us landmarks in the blackness
    and we think of Christ.

Thank you for hope.
Some day the eastern heavens will pour gold and color and
warmth over the whole earth and all the weeping
    will turn to laughter.
        We are busy
            we are waiting and
        until the moment when
        hope comes into its own
            triumphant,
    we thank you that we are sustained by
        love
            and work
                and prayer
                    and faith in you.
We are destined to worship you—on that day as now
    and to tell our story
        not of patient endurance
        but of glorifying God
            and enjoying Him forever.

PRAYER FOR EXTREMELY BUSY PEOPLE

Eternal Creator, Lord of this and every place,
of this and every time,
we see the faces of new students here,
and we sense how swift are the cycles of life.
Since we are born to be children of time
we yield to it, often with celebration,
more often with painful remorse.
Our Lord, this week we ask a special favor of you,
to stop the clock and hold a moment still
for thanksgiving.
Nothing we know of in science or experience is so fast
as the growth of our children.
For a moment now and then let us see and feel and
know them as they are.
Enable us to genuinely see and hear
members of the family, neighbors,
persons we work with, fellow and sister students,
that we may live richly and thankfully,
even for a moment.
Help us to pause at a meal and make it church.
Grant us a minute to inform an old enemy that
bygones are bygones, or perhaps tell an old friend
"I love you."
For Lord, we are making memories with you that
we shall leaf through for eternity,
and we ask you to help us make eternity
an experience of resolution and joy
and not a place marred by regret.
Now is the short time we are to know you as people,
to love you through all change,
to learn some of your ways with us, and
to live the measured pace of life eternal before
we the family are reunited in the New Jerusalem.
Through Jesus Christ our Lord, Amen.

A Prayer for Persistence

Our God, president of the universe
and executive director of human affairs,
our prayer this morning is for those
tempted to yield to defeat: Press on.
Grant them strength to press on.
When our cherished dreams begin to burst
like children's bubbles blown to the air,
when people of common sense and clear sight,
when doctors and lawyers, specialists, friends
and neighbors all cry:
"A good try, but you're through."
Lord, give us strength to keep on persisting.
Light the fire to press on.
When a handicap almost eliminates us,
or a failing business embarrasses us,
when a good marriage turns sour,
and people of good will counsel to face reality,
give up, and start again another day,
Lord, save us from well-meant advice.
With painful, unremitting, dogged determination,
despite our moaning and groaning,
forsake your perfectly clear foreknowledge for awhile,
join our foolish cause,
and blow the trumpet to press on.
And when the forces are overwhelming—
as in illness or death—
keep our goal ever before us—
defiantly—past every temporary setback,
past every discouragement,
past every surrender of those we love and respect,
give us the mighty power of God to press on
and on
and on.
Through Jesus Christ our Lord, Amen.

THE COMPANIONSHIP OF GOD

Our Father-Creator, who pronounced a universe into existence,
who spoke "Adam" and staged the human play,
who said "Eve" and created love, who sent your Son
to a tiny planet and received Him back
  with many friends;
We testify to all in heaven and earth that you are the ultimate
world to us and the reason for our being.

Above all things, for the thirty-three years Jesus walked among
us, and that now we are always on His mind.

  Thank you.

Your presence is both joy and assurance.
We know that in every trip
  you are the first to greet us,
  the last to say Good-bye.
Every meal will be a Eucharist, and in every happiness
  we hear your laughter.
In every suffering we shall feel your pain;
  in every waiting we shall hear your quietness.
Into our common sense you pour your wisdom;
  to our faltering strength you lend your power.
Your silence assures us that for some mysteries
  there are no answers.

We do not ask to be liberated from our flesh and blood,
but only to be spared the betrayal which sees
our humanity as an excuse instead of our nobility.

Lord, we celebrate our humanity lavishly, our feelings, our
dreams and aspirations, our love, our capacity to be wounded
    and to be healed;
    our working hard and our sleeping restfully;
For all we are have become divine metaphors
for your attributes;
    and we have taken our place with Jesus, a person
        just like us.
We the people long for the sights and sounds of you even
though we know you are here. If you care to, make a little
recognizable noise when people laugh, or perhaps
    suggest a favorite hymn of yours we may hum,
        or prompt us to memorize Psalm 103;
            or some night whisper something in plain English;
                or if you decide to converse through a friend,
                    that's all right too.

At the moment of death when we hear the rustle of a wing,
we need also to hear from you a sound, just a sight or a sound.
    King of the ages, you are sufficient for this life.
    And when you promised, "I shall never leave you
        or forsake you," you answered every prayer
we shall ever pray.

In Christ's name, Amen.

FOR WHAT WE KNOW

Before you, the people will rejoice, O God,
   and express gratitude
   with all the power of our being.
We have experienced your riches, and your riches are
   the impetus for living and
   the fabric of our worship.
We know your truth is true
   even though we deface it.
We know your inexpressible generosity, even though
   millions of our children perish from hunger.
We know of your inescapable justice even though
   tyrants oppress, and madmen steal.
We know of your grace even though
   oppression stalks the world and
   hopelessness defiles sacred dreams.
We know the infinite goodness of Jesus Christ, our Lord,
   even though so many surrender to alienation.
We know of the mighty, pealing, ringing,
   resurrection power already at work, even though
   our very neighbors stare into the future with terror.
As we rejoice for the life—nourishing sun even when
   hidden by clouds, so we raise anthems of praise to you
   even when your reality is blurred by suffering.

Hallelujah for the Presence of Christ among the poor.
Hallelujah, O Christ,
   for taking our condition upon yourself
   that we might make the condition of others our own.

Hallelujah, O God, for the truth nevertheless.
Hallelujah, Amen.

SIGNIFICANCE THROUGH SUFFERING

Lord God, high and lifted up above the world's vanities,
    we confess our commitment to being victims.
We secretly cherish all the slings and arrows of
    misfortune that have wounded us.
Not for a moment do we intend to forget
    the disappointments, betrayals, insults,
    defeats and embarrassments inflicted on us
    by family, friend, neighbor, and
    brother and sister Christians.
Oh, how good they feel!
Now we can cherish our wounds
    because we have been victimized.
We wear the badge of the persecuted ones.
We, like Jesus, have suffered.
There are people out there who owe us.
We victims are entitled to special grace,
    special sympathy, special consideration, and
    an addenda in Fox's Book of Martyrs.
The fact that we choose to be victims, and
    that Paul said we are actually more than conquerors
    through Him who loved us
    is a distraction.
For the few who are thoroughly disenchanted
    with this wretched role, we confess it
    in behalf of our own true strength and for the good
    of all those we have tyrannized.
And our sincerity, O Lord God, will be gauged
    by our willingness to relinquish it.
In the name of Christ who breaths into us forgiveness
    and not punishment
We confess our sin to you and others so afflicted.
    Amen.

As a Child Sees it

Lord, Master of the affairs of people and of angels,
Manager of our solar system and guardian of our souls,
King of Kings and Lord of Lords and friend
of the greatest and the least of us,
we pray for the children,
and those who devote their lives to them.
Today we would lift up the prayers of the children.

Father, we thank you for our mothers and fathers,
for all they do for us,
and for being so happy just because we brush our teeth
and come home on time.
They get cranky at times, but that's all right;
tell them to keep up the good work.
God, here's a prayer for my teachers.
Please tell my arithmetic teacher not to blow up at me.
Help her see I'm only brain damaged in math, and
I'm really a fine person.

And I'm glad that Jesus must be
like my sports coach.
I can talk to him when I'm confused, and
he certainly knows what works,
and what doesn't.
I'm sure he must pray for all us kids,
so be sure to answer his prayers.

God, help me be a friend
to the new children at school,
especially those from strange countries
that I didn't know existed.
They look alone and shy, like I feel sometimes.
And just like mother never minds loads of company
—she says she doesn't—
so help us welcome these guests to our land
who look like they intend to stay.
There's room, Jesus, just like there's room
in your heart for everyone.
Please bless, my brothers and sisters, and
especially the children with no home like ours.

And in conclusion I'd like to say, I'm happy you're God,
just as I'm sure you're happy I'm me.
In Jesus name, Amen.

THE BOND WITH GOD

Lord God, hear our prayer, and grant us
    the gift of faith.
Grant us the faith to see your majestic glory
    when our eyes are blinded by your invisibility.
Grant us the faith to verify again and again,
    the death and resurrection of Jesus Christ
    as the event of our union with you here and now.
We seek faith for significance.
Help us to believe if we turn off the television
we shall not fall into a black, bottomless pit.
Help us trust that we were destined
    for excellent reading
        stimulating conversation,
            faithful friendship,
                and to be a Good Samaritan to those
                who need a helping hand.
There are some here
    who have experienced shattering storms
    and a few shipwrecks.
Give them a sign, a whispered word,
    a verse of scripture, the echo of a friend,
    the memory of a lighted moment
    to brace their spine.
May faith be theirs now
    to look beyond their day's calamity
    to tomorrow's wisdom and
    new opportunities.
We believe your love will never let us go—
We say with the disciples—Lord, increase our faith.
And should goodness and caring join hands,
we want to say to others as we have said to ourselves.
Have faith in God. In Jesus name we pray. Amen.

EASTER

Good morning, Lord Jesus,
it's a marvelous celebration.
It's the time for singing, smiling
and hearty laughing, and story-telling.
Like the time ol' death, billed as the invincible ghost,
went to pick up someone in Jerusalem
early one Sunday morning,
and it turned out to be Jesus.
What a shock!

What a surprise to learn that *his* time was up, and that
The Savior who appears in the Sunday School lessons
as the meek and mild lover of children
could be the Leader of Humanity,
the President of Heaven and Earth.
Lord, to us Easter means that Christ
the Life is here forever.

EASTER PRAYER

Hail to thee, sovereign of life, and Lord of the world,
  on this day when Christ the King engages
  all the foes that have ever killed us,
    ranged deeply into hell on our behalf, and
    returned, covered with glory.

If you never hear another prayer from us,
Remember that we said,
"Our God, thank you for life."

It is with horror that we see how
    we still die in small pieces.
  It is not the great transition we fear, O Lord,
    it is slowly dying in resentment,
    in loneliness, in wounds that never heal,
    in petty vengeance far beneath us, and
    in grief that our long-held investments
      in safety and security
          never
            paid
              off.
May our love rise from the ashes of death
  in other forms
You have snared us with life,
  now march with us into the persistence
  of faith, and a new dawn as
  Easter morning.

30

We who often ask, "What is God doing?" know full well
  what you have done, and are doing.
The question is: "What are we doing, O God?"

Sound the trumpets every day so that we shall march out
  with Christ, and the news Christ is risen shall
  reverberate in the hospital corridors
  where our people are desperately ill;
      echo out into the cities where men and women
      and little ones are crippled by injustice;
          out into the prisons of the world where people rot
          awaiting news from somewhere;
              far into the countryside where your people
              are dying from hunger—hunger for bread,
              hunger for peace—

  O God forgive us
but the battle cannot be fully won for us
until it is won for everyone,
  and those awaiting freedom from death and folly,
  and injustice
hear the cry CHRIST IS RISEN! and turn to their neighbor
  and proclaim
          CHRIST IS RISEN!
and discover in an awesome anthem of triumph
  for the people, OH YES, HE IS RISEN INDEED!
For this day, great God, and for the one to come,
  we sing:
          HALLELUJAH!

FRIEND AND LORD

We need your Spirit to prompt us with "Christ is risen" when
we have the power to share life and happiness with another.

We need to hear "Encouraging Easter" when our grades are
slipping and everywhere there's work, work, work—

And to hear "Good morning, it's Easter," when we wake up at
fifty and feel we're going nowhere.

—to hear "Have a blessed Easter" when we are fired
from our job;

—and to hear "Easter power!" when we are working on our
marriage and it's taking too long.

We need to hear "Christ fought with death and defeated him"
when we dabble with some temptation that could *never* be
worth it.

To these and others, send us with Gospel shouts:
       COME, COME to the laughter!
  It's a party of life
       AND YOU'RE INVITED
            signed,
              The Lord Jesus Christ.

EUCHARIST

Before hands touch across the aisles
  and hearts link across eternity,
  we raise the bread and wine
  for your blessing of holiness.

As the elements of earth become part
  of every earthly cell, so may now, O God,
  the life of the Lord Jesus Christ fulfill
  every cell of our being.

May the authority of Christ be woven into our will;
  the Spirit's breath of inspiration fill our hearts,
  the eternal law of justice and honor
  be chiseled into our minds,
  and the Creator's love for all humankind
  mold our vision of the good life.

Since the homeless poor are not at table—may they be.
If the oppressed cannot hear word of their liberation here—
may they hear it somewhere—
  so that one day every seat may be taken
  and the family—your sons and daughters—
  may be complete.

O, my Lord, what a day of glory *that will be*.
  Through Christ our Lord. Amen.

Prayer for a Life Not Marred by Regrets

Father and God of all that lives, who is the
essence of power and who singularly prizes our freedom,
grant us a bold life not marred by regret.

All the ingredients of our happiness are before us.
We lack nothing for the courageous sculpting of our future.
We constantly complain that we need more and bigger and
finer, or we are handicapped. We look back, O God, and
realize we have always had what we required from you for a
significant and satisfying life. The opportunities for enriching
others did not always seem attractive nor the call to shoulder
the cross seem so compelling at the time. A later unfolding of
our drama revealed the patient movement of a hidden hand.
Just beneath the surface of things you have always been
enticing us on to a better way.

We resist you to our sorrow. "It is too late," we complain.
"If only I had done this, or decided to do that,
or taken another road back then,
or chose others to live with . . . why then . . ."

Wisdom has taught us the futility, O God, of forfeiting the power of home and the exhilaration of plans because of past mistakes. Actually, Father, we keep the past alive so that it can continue to excuse us from all the exciting participation in love and life that each year should bring.

We implore you now to graciously bury yesterday's futility so that we may retrieve our lessons, and cherish blessings forgotten so soon.

Grant that as long as we live, in whatever crisis we find ourselves, no matter how pressed for hope, no matter how disillusion we are over the drama we wrote, we shall always hear resounding throughout the sanctuary of our souls, the mighty and timely affirmation of a person like us: "I can do all things through Him who strengthens me."

This, Lord, we believe. By your patience, this we shall live.

Through Christ our Lord. Amen.

A PRAYER FOR FEELING GOOD

Great God whose power to create is greater
   than we can imagine,
and whose compassion is far greater
   than we could ever experience—
   we address you with confidence and poise.
We are basically a good people
   who have made our share of mistakes.
We confess to you our regrets, but not our sins.
We want to share our remorse without guilt.
We regret that we have taken loved ones for granted.
   We were always so busy . . .
We regret in the grand scheme of things
   life was lived on the wheel of routine and
   not in the high seas of exploration and discovery.
We regret that while we know more than we know,
   we are not as smart as we think,
   that we hoarded our powers,
   lost ourselves in petty distractions,
   kept ourselves a secret,
   married TV at an early age,
And spent so little time in the service of our nation.
We regret that we have learned so little
   from our friends, especially our children.
The waves of time erode our shores
   and we are sorry that some of our fondest dreams
   are buried in sand.
And while you are the God
   who arises anew with each dawn,
   still it is a priceless comfort to read you our diaries without
   feeling like failures or pleading for mercy.
We are what we are, and for all that we would like
   to feel your acceptance and satisfaction—
   without regret.
Through Christ our Lord. Amen.

THE SAINTS GO MARCHING IN

God of all beauty who illumines the heavens and provides a
shelter in eternity, we thank you for music.
You are the conductor of the symphony,
the music of the rolling spheres.
As a conductor raises his or her baton,
so you send music at noon or midnight
when it is a miracle to us that you know where we are.
A magnificent profusion of goodness pours out upon us.
While other pilgrims hear only a mocking silence
we hear the trumpets in the morning,
martial music at midday,
and the grace notes of perfect peace at day's end.
We are grateful for the inspiring crescendos
when wisdom is clear,
and now and then we hear a mighty anthem of faith
as we march to the frontier with Christ.

At times we hear the resurrection strains
of Dixieland Jazz and at others
we hear the funeral dirges of those families
living and dying on our city streets.
Often we do not understand the meaning
but we feel the refrain of high praise
defying insignificance and death.
We long for the day of harmony,
when all shall be attuned to Christ,
and men and women, boys and girls,
and those living in luxury, and those
in the city's streets,
shall all hear the Gospel music and
join in a resounding chorus of thanksgiving.
Bless the Lord O my soul and all that is within me,
bless his holy name. Amen.

THE MADNESS OF WAR

"O God, our help in ages past,
Our hope for years to come,
Our shelter from the stormy blast,
and Our eternal home."

Today we remember, we remember you as the author
of our sacred documents,
and the parent of all the people of this, our land.
Your dedication to justice is boundless, and
your faithfulness to this people has been untarnished.

We are profoundly thankful for the sacrifice of your son,
for liberation and peace,
as we are thankful for the gift of
our sons and daughters to you
on the sacrificial altar of freedom and justice.
We would honor you for our spirit of reconciliation
after our wars.

Likewise, we would like to say that our hearts are pure,
and our great nation has
never taken the land of another,
or needlessly humbled its people.

38

To our eternal sorrow we cannot say that, O Lord,
   and we too are afflicted with the inherited psychosis
   of the human race:

   the madness of war.

May we together put forth every effort,
   in every way, at every time,
      with every opportunity to make our strength
         known eloquently for peace and for justice, and
            may we, your sons and daughters,
      never become passive in the shadow of the bomb,
   lest they say, "See, their God is helpless."

But instead shall say:
      "They shall beat their swords into plowshares,
      and their spears into pruning hooks;
      nation shall not lift up sword against nation,
      neither shall they learn war any more" (Isaiah 2:4).

                    Amen.

WHERE IS JESUS?

God of all power and love, Lord of all people,
God who is our parents, our Savior and our Holy Spirit,
In respect and devotion
we confess this morning the oldest sin in the books:
remaking you into our image.

We look around and everyone looks the same.
We confess our lapses from middle class respectability
  in the name of the one born of peasants, dark-skinned,
  unemployed, transient, poor, and
  with no permanent address.
We wonder if Jesus would be welcome
  in this congregation.

As we look around we shall not ask
  if his friends feel welcome.
Apparently, O Lord, this is our Gospel: come to Jesus
  who looks like a white person in East Bay, California.
We are proud, Father, that Jesus knows
  where he can find us—in the sanctuary.
We are occasionally embarrassed to remember,
  where we can find Jesus—out in the streets
    with the people.

Eternal Creator, we wish to remember that
  we do not look like you, and you do not look like us.
We would confess that as a minority, we practice a minority
Gospel with minor appeal.

We would confess our sin of singing
  Jesus loves *me*, and *mine* and *ours*,
and repent while singing
  Jesus loves the little children,
  all the children of the world,
  red and yellow, black and white,
  they are precious in His sight,
  Jesus loves the little children of the world.

Let us receive the assurance:

May the Blood of Christ as a Lamb
  without blemish and without spot,
  cover our hearts with the mercy of God,
  absolving us from all our sins,
  and granting us His peace.

Amen.

Prayer for Fairly Righteous Folks

Our eternal and omnipotent God,
  we anticipate the public confession of our sins
  with the least enthusiasm.
Our healers have taught us that only deep appreciation
  and love for ourselves will enable us
  to traverse our destiny, with great strides.
And yet, in light of the Gospel of Christ, we confess
  that few of us surpass average,
  middle class respectability.
Our confession is not that we do not know the Gospel,
  but that we have so little to show for it.
And so we shall always be making confessions
  so that we may hear your Word.
We shall probably always repeat
  much of the same old thing;
Our friendship with Jesus
  remains the heart of our greatness.
Whoever expects us to be perfect, our Lord,
  is no friend of ours.
We want to be honest with you, so we may claim,
  the grandeur of being human.
And, O Lord, we want always to come in open confession
  in the house of our God, so that when one of us
  does a stupid thing, and falters, he may be
  lifted to his feet by those who understand.
Almighty God, who does freely pardon all who repent and
  turn to Him, now fulfill in every contrite heart the promise
  of redeeming grace; remitting all our sins,
  and cleansing us from an evil conscience;
  through the sacrifice of Christ in His glorious death
  and resurrection.
In Christ's name.   Amen.

PRAYER FOR THE BREATH OF LIFE

Creator, we honor and worship you.
We ask what it is you are most desirous of granting us.
We pray that you breathe life into us.
Grant to youth life in its enthusiasm and
high expectations, its dreams and hope without limits.
Grant life in the middle years, times to pause,
and linger in love;
the days when time is splintered to the winds
and leaves us quickly.
Grant life to be fruitful before the harvest.
Give life to the fruitful years
when truth seizes us that suddenly
the children are grown,
happiness did not come with money,
we shall not achieve quite what we had hoped for,
and our mission for Christ was forever postponed.
Grant us to move with the tides of life,
to speak gently to ourselves and others,
and to discover the joys of living
beyond life's elusive prizes.
Grant to these times, O Lord,
life in a cleared agenda, new priorities,
a new message for family and friends,
and a new romance with all things fresh and lively.
Grant life to later years, O Lord,
a time for breaking open the universe as a fruit,
when the unspeakable glory of the New Jerusalem,
our eternal home, is spread before us.
We who have heard the rustle of an angel's wing
would listen instead for the sound of the trumpet,
when your Son shall return and the dead in Christ
shall come into life, and the family circle
is unbroken at last.
We look forward to that day of life, O Lord.
Doubtless . . . a day just like today. In Christ's name.

THE SANCTITY OF ORDINARY THINGS

Lord God who reigns supreme over all people,
in all lands, through all time and change,
whose love does not vary with history,
and whose power is not diminished by human recklessness,
we ask you now to touch the ordinary things of life
to make them sacred.

We are greatly challenged to high adventure in Christ.
We are rallied to witness, preach, teach, travel,
and be outstanding. We hear the summons
but many cannot respond just now.
Lord, there are children to dress, business to complete,
bills to pay, letters to write, houses to clean
groceries to buy, neighbors to visit, and
holidays to celebrate.
The one question we persistently ask life is:
Where did the time go?

We do not ask to escape our tasks, nor evade
our vital obligations.
We do ask you to lay your hand of holiness and blessing
upon all the ordinary things we must do
merely to stay alive and sane in urban life.

Provide us the assurance just now that in your eyes
our work is indeed a divine work,
and that we are called to do routine work
with satisfaction and joy.
We need confidence from time to time
that as we have made your labor ours,
so you have made our labor yours.

Consecrate our desks as meeting places with you,
our kitchen sink as an altar where prayers are lifted up
and our table as a Eucharist
where we also commune with Jesus Christ.
We know that wherever we are, we are with Christ
who lived among the people and did mighty acts of God
where they lived.
So now we are conscious that this same Christ
touches all things and makes them sacred.

Grant that we shall live in this spirit of holiness.

In the name of Christ we pray.

Amen .

A Prayer for Our Hearing Loss

O Lord, we admit to you that we are
becoming hard of hearing at a tender age.
Our children have something to say to us,
    but we can't hear them.
Spouses have a message or two,
    but they are unable to get through.
Friends would like to be more authentic with us,
    but they don't dare.
The preacher speaks from the word
and he means the ones sitting next to us . . .
    we hope they hear it.
Our neighbors have a message we could use,
    but they seem to be strange people
        so no need to hear it.
Lord, guide our hand up to our ears and
    slowly remove this screen by which
    flattery and delightful news gets through
    and anything else is censored.
We never want that terrible question of Christ
    addressed to us as well as the Pharisees:
Lord, open our ears,
    then our eyes,
      then our hearts,
        our time,
         our plans,
           our pocketbook,
             our lives.
Lord, open everything. In Christ's name.
Amen.

PRAYER FOR THE DEDICATION OF A HOME

My north star is the light of one candle
  which has been
    and will be

                a light of invitation when weary
          a light of hope when defeated
        a light of refuge from crashing storms
       a light from eternity on the grave's gray rim
      a light unfailing as the love of God

Do you see it, too?

Follow me, and make this light ours,
For when we reach it,
All will be well,

      to laugh
        or cry
          or sleep
            or plan or eat
            or love

For it is my sacred place, and yours as well.

This is our home. In Christ's love.

Amen.

A Prayer for Liberation

Lord, high and lifted up above human folly,
    but boundless in mercy and compassion:

This sin is so great and destructive
    we hesitate to broach the subject
    in a short prayer.

I have reference to America's seduction
    by the TV box.

Time is so short. Like an ever-rolling stream
    it bears our sons and daughters away
    while we stare from forty to fifty hours a week
    into the box.

While life reduces us to utter chaos, our hope is
    that our favorite show will not be cancelled.

We who are in desperate need of a working theology
    know we shall find it on Cagney and Lacey
    if we keep looking for their reruns.

And while we all struggle for significance
    a million years from now, the only thing
    we'll remember is the forth rerun of
    of Golden Girls in weekly episodes.

No doubt someone will approach you to plead
    that TV is just a neutral device and
    only people can be evil.

Don't listen to him Lord; he's an addict.
    They said the serpent was
    just a harmless little snake
    and look at us now.

The box is inherently bad, Lord, every tube, circuit,
    every cathode and wire—
    all an instrument of the devil.

The situation is so desperate that I can
    think of no request, expect no guilt,
    repentance or grace and have no hope.

And so while a few of us will prepare for Armageddon,
    that glorious and decisive struggle
    for world control by forces
    of good and evil—
    —the rest will slip silently into
    the stream of eternity, hypnotized into
    mindlessness by our own electronic gadgets.

Lord, help us to wake up and experience
    the incredible realities of
    your beautiful earth first hand.
    In Jesus name. Amen.

GIVE US A CAUSE

Our Eternal Lord God,
Silent Sovereign in the affairs of humankind,
and that's not the half of it, merciful Father,
Parent Forever of His frail but noble children;
grant us the thrill of investing our eternal life
in causes that shall outlive us.

As it is we trivialize the hours
as if time were cheaper than air.
We spend so much time keeping our heads above water
that our ship never leaves port.
True, we have kept our reputation untarnished,
and have amassed a lavish display of merit badges
in Church achievement;
We have our charities,
our myriad duties in behalf of home and club,
and we speak up righteously for those pale virtues
least likely to bestir controversy.
Fortunately, we are blessed with television
by which we kill time before it becomes a glut.

Lord, we suffer most from our absence of great careers
but none that appeal to our wholehearted enlistment.
Put a fire under our feelings
until we leave the shadows of mediocrity to
walk with Christ into unchartered days.
Grant us a preview again of the world as Jesus sees it.

Open our eyes to the holocausts in the Middle East,
Ethiopia, the Sudan, Afghanistan, Nicaragua.
May our nerves be rubbed raw by the sight of tyranny,
the expressionless faces in Berkeley,
the homeless people always shuffling,
always on the move, the alcoholics,
the ones terribly ill and too poor for treatment,
the hidden elderly ones, the children,
battered, lost and terrified.

Lord, in this rich land we have so much time, power,
skill and love which are simply not mobilized.
We need causes that will drain us, count on us,
cost us, make us forget merry-go-round living,
that take us by the heart and throw us into the action
where God is fighting for His people.

We need, O Lord, excitement,
scars for people not our relatives,
prayers for people we could ignore,
we need shouts, great songs of victory
and yells of joy for healing and new birth,
of justice and new liberty for people who would mean
nothing to us if it were not for Christ.
Lord God, give us a great cause.
We'll never experience your power, know the joy,
test the hope, realize the full truth
unless we seize the hour and cry,
"Here am I—"
Lord, God, grant us a great cause now.
In Jesus name,
Amen

GIFT OF MEANING

Lord God, who knows the course of every atom
    since creation
and clearly every biography from the homeless,
    to the high and mighty
    to the down and out,
receive our adoration this morning
especially from those here who have been
baptized by a new visitation of significance.

For too long we felt insignificant.
It was not clear whether you ran the world or we did.
We tried to find significance
    by printing its counterfeit prestige.
And we not only worked desperately
at putting on perfectionism,
and telling everyone how to live,
but we asked your help to succeed.

How does it feel when one half the church
asks you to bless their efforts
to manipulate and control the other half?
All for their mutual benefit!

Our efforts at finding significance have entrapped us
    in petty superiority and unending frustration.
Lord, may the freedom lovers, by your Spirit, resist
    every attempt at tying up our liberty in Christ.

You created, justified, redeemed, and incorporated us
        into a world dignified by your Spirit
                and assured us of eternal life.
So, Lord, what is this need for pretense
        instead of grace.
Lord, in our prayer life enable us to focus in on
        what gives us significance of the covenant
                "in Christ."
Help us to diligently check our work, our relationships,
        our honesty, our capacity to love graciously, and
        our service to you among people
inside and outside this church building.

We promise to drop what demeans us,
        that which leaves us feeling small, useless.
Instead enable us to retrain our thinking
        to visit, to laugh, to meditate, to befriend,
        to dare, to believe, to picture Christ,
        to talk to you, and to think a lot about
            all those lovely things in Philippians 4.

We are all at a different station
    in the unfair world, O Lord,
Thus, Father, we adore you
        for our eternal meaning.

And because it feels so good to say it,
we shall repeat it,
The children of the living God.

In Christ's name. Amen.

ARE YOU THERE, GOD?

Great God, shattering the bounds of imagination,
Who brought all reality into Being, but is unseen;
  Come and reveal yourself more fully.

In the sorrows and anguish, in life and in death,
 our consolation is "Thou are with me."
  Your stern rule and companionship,
   your terrible judgments and tender compassion
    are the mainstay of our pilgrim journey.

But if you are our all in all, we ask,
 Who and where are you God?"
  You speak, but we hear nothing.
   You send light, and we see shadows.
    We feel your hands on our sick and suffering ones.
But these look like human hands.

We pray, experience a flash of joy,
 look up expecting to see your face
  and see instead our spouse
   or a ray of window light
    or an ecstatic child whose spirit is not yet broken
     or a strong, old tree.

The truth is that we must think of you as Jesus,
O God, else how can we love you?
We forgive you for the terrible suffering,
 for those who never really lived,
  for the humiliation of the homeless
   the flickering candle of those starving,
but we need to touch you,
 friend to friend,
  person to Jesus,
   disciple to teacher,
else how can we argue with you?
And complain, and struggle, and get angry?

We know you are not a human being,
   but we must embrace you,
    and communicate and close the gap.
We are brilliant creatures, O Lord,
   but with very small minds
and so when we sing, "Jesus is all the world to me"
   you must know that we can only take comfort
        in a God of human experience.
Through all time and change, O God, and in every place,
   we pray to know a deep peace
    when we say, "Have faith in God."
In the name of Him who declared,
    "He that has seen me has seen the Father,"
        our Lord Jesus Christ, we pray,
Amen.

A House Is an Incarnation

A House
  Like Christ our Lord
    Is the incarnation of Spirit
Like the hues of Spring
    too sensitive for sight
Like the fragrance of summer
    too subtle to feel.
An emanation seeking neighborhood
  spreads slowly, and attracts.
A home becomes a spirit
  where people find a habitat
    a place of comfort
      an on-the-way house
              more than an address
              more than a residence
  where they smile and talk
    for they belong.

A home is, like Christ,
  an incarnation of love
    a rendezvous of care and rest
a place of rootedness,
    for eating
      and drinking
          and telling long stories half true
            and laughing for the fun of it.

A home must be baptized to destiny
  as was Christ,
    for there will be times when laughter
        turns to tears
    and the stories are true
    and life is measured by truth uncovered.

I would like such a home
  an incarnation of the spirit
  where lives cross, and recross
    and sense that any one of us—
    or all of us—
  are the presence of Jesus.
        Who knows?

But this I know
  as the arms of the Word made flesh enfold you
    So may the welcome of this house;
        And if you make it your home,
        It shall be mine as well.

In Jesus' precious love, Amen.

PRAYER FOR A TICKLED FANCY

Lord, sovereign Creator who works in every act
for our sake;
you are fully present to every living thing.
We have no sense to see you,
no faculty to imagine you, and no words to express you.

Yet our hearts are filled with you.
Thank you for living within human experience
and speaking to us in silence, miracles, mystery,
and plain English.
We who were created from the dust
petition you to make us earthy pilgrims
with a down-to-earth way about us.
Grant us an August celebration of creation
when the earth goes to a party in a riot of color.
Help us to feel the texture,
not merely touch the surface.

Tickle our fancy so that we praise you
with deep, long howls of laughter,
not these little tee hees we hear.
Instead of waiting, ever waiting for who knows what,
edge us out there to risk what we have—
now—all of it.
Instead of staring at re-runs,
entice us somehow to move out where something is new,
and look into it—appreciatively.

Not tomorrow, but today,
bring us a new excitement
about every loved one we take for granted
so we can get reacquainted.

Expand our lungs for deep breaths of precious air,
and expand our hearts for deep feelings,
heart-pounding excitement,
loud singing either on or off key,
and love-filled passion besides.

Expand our minds, O God,
to keep company with great thoughts,
whether or not we understand them,
so that sooner or later all shall be amazed when we say
something original.
Picture Jesus the Carpenter to us,
the Man of the people, so that we can do
something for the weak, someone bored, or grieving,
or lonely, sick, lost, or just needing a friend,
anything for someone besides ourselves.

Grant us to cooperate with the circling times
and seasons, O Lord, from winter to harvest,
giving you high praise for it all,
so that when this life is over
we can say with a satisfied smile that we lived it.
In Jesus name,
Amen.

PRAYER AT ORDINATION

O Lord Jesus Christ, we the people give you
one of us to be your flesh and blood in these
days of terror and nights of restlessness.
Nations suffering from confusion and hunger
have committed themselves to war.
The lights flicker in our beloved nation,
and even the church raises a trumpet of uncertain sound.

If ever we needed you to be the Savior for all humankind,
it is now.

If ever we needed the Gospel in the gracious truth of
Word made flesh,
it is today.

If ever we the people needed to experience
your almighty power, your tender faithfulness,
your healing embrace, your light of hope,
and the inspiration of enthusiasm in song
dance, and celebration,
it is this very hour.

As you walked, taught, healed, listened, and gave
new beginnings for men and women to know again
the honor, the dignity, the royalty of being human,
so be your very same self in this world, and this city,
for the sake of the people.

And may your newly committed servant pastor
walk and talk where you are,
heal and preach as you do,
listen and pray in your way,
so that over the years we the people will come to
know you as a greater unending reality
than the days of terror and the nights of restlessness.
We thank you for yourself and for him.
Those who shall know the hand of Christ again
thank you. His family thank you.
The pastors and teachers who invested
their very life blood in him thank you.
Those who need the Gospel more than food and drink
thank you. And above all we thank you
for sharing your breath of life with ministers,
all ordained in their baptism,
that we are able to do in this world for others
what we could never, in our own power, do for ourselves.
Yes, we the people thank you, O Christ.
We the children of God praise you.
We, your very body, shout to you: Hallelujah.
Hallelujah. Hallelujah.
In the name of the Father, the Son,
and the Holy Spirit.
Amen.

A PRAYER FOR LIGHT

O God who said, "Let light shine out of darkness,"
and has shone in our hearts
to give the light of the knowledge
of the glory of God in the face of Christ,
turn on the lights again in our dark places.
There are some in this room
who silently suffer the pain of loneliness and
the fear of being rejected
by love itself.
The softest radiance would comfort,
and your Spirit recruiting a sharing friend
can bring light.
For some cause quite unreasonable some of us here,
O God, suffer a spiritual drought.
The strings of the heart are broken or out of tune,
and we complain anxiously: No joy,
no late night parties with the Lord, Jesus Christ,
No music, no wisdom, no laughter, no God.
All is gray too soon, and
we miss the brightness.
Would you believe, our Father,
that some in this very room
have taken to generate counterfeit happiness.
They have not been truthful in their marriage and
some have started illicit affairs and
a dark and unholy shattering of the sacred covenant.

Don't ask us how we know.
These benighted souls in search of love
need to become genuine again.
When they realize how much time they must spend
in the darkness to avoid you, speak an invitation to
them, for your Word is light.
We are all discrete about our preference for the dark,
O Lord, and we avoid criticism, evaluation, feedback,
testing, or any means of exposing
the depths of the heart to the intensity of your truth.
This week may there be a baptism
of Springtime for your people.
Sound the trumpet and raise us early,
so when the eastern sun pours its warmth and joy,
color and resounding radiance over the whole world
we may, with open arms, welcome the dawn and cry,
"Lord God of earth,
my God,
turn on the light once more."

Through Jesus Christ, our Lord.

Amen.

OUR PRAYER FOR PEOPLE WHO ARE STUCK

Lord God of the rolling spheres,
Creator of all eternity, and
Architect of human life:
Receive our thanksgiving for your intervention
  in our world in behalf of the people.
You have given us the courage to face life
  and make it worth living.

Unfortunately, we have come to expect special privileges,
and become petulantly angry when they are not forthcoming.

We are angry that God could have
  healed our depression and didn't;
could have saved a bad marriage,
  and apparently chose not to;
could have saved Aunt Mary from dying and didn't;
could have saved the space shuttle astronauts
  from being destroyed, and did not.

Our prayer is that you will enable us to be
  partners with you in the work of the ministry.
Channel our anger into something decent —
  like hard work.

If we are angry that no one visited us,
   remind us to visit.
If we are feeling sorry for ourselves,
   send us out to feel sorry for someone else.
If we are waiting for your hands to cure,
   send us out to cure, using our own.
Grant us to find someone as miserable as we are.
We who are alone need a party to crash,
   a stranger to visit, and
      a neighbor to meet.

We who are waiting for a miracle
      need to imitate one.
Those here waiting for a revelation of your will
      need to do what they know.
Those who complain about what you aren't doing
         need to go and find you what you are doing.
Enable us to take full responsibility not for—
   but in the Kingdom of God, and
   expect from us full cooperation
   in answering our prayers.

Through Christ our Lord. Amen.

CONFESSION OF EXCUSES

Our Lord God and Savior,
Sovereign power over all powers, and
Authority over all authorities,
We spread before your eyes the excuses
  which explain why we are unfulfilled.
Here now on your altar are the tried and true reasons
  why we are frustrated.
We know how duly impressed you are
  with the psychological theories which
  point out the hangups of our parents, and
  the relentless rivalry of our brothers and sisters.
Our wisdom now understands the
  ineptness of our teachers,
  the futility of the church,
  the unneighborliness of our neighbors, and
  the pressure of our peers
  which forces us into it.
And, too often, no explanations are needed.
Some here are unfortunately over forty years of age, and
  probably some are even older,
  and there you are, right there.
And you allowed some people to be overly tall,
  and others, even worse,
  to be shorter than everyone else.

Some here are, as you can see plain looking,
    and others, well, tend to be a bit ugly.
Others, Lord, were divinely chosen to see
    how much misfortune they could endure
    before giving in.
It's not an easy thing being a victim day in and day out.
And on top of it, we are not sure,
    with prayers like this,
    that anyone is still listening.
Lord, the thought of the Almighty
    yawning over our poor excuses
    ought to be terrifying.

Sweep the altar clean of pitiful reasons,
Grant us the power of your Holy Spirit,
Give us the courage to stand straight ourselves,
And to reach out in partnership to the handicapped,
    and may there be nothing between us
Except the truth of a new day.

Shalom!

In the name of the Father, the Son, and the Holy Spirit.

Amen.

HELP US TO DO WHAT YOU REQUIRE

Great God who made everything beyond our knowledge,
  who is before the beginning and after the ending,
  inspire in us new confidence
to create beyond our knowledge and
love beyond our limits.

Over the years we have become distressed with those
  we could not love.
We could not be expected to forgive *that* relative
  or reasonably be expected to love that neighbor;
    and no one with any sense could forgive
    that alleged friend,
And as for that person who divorced us—
    (just up and abandoned us)
Well, only God knows the anguish—the torture.
How could I forgive and maintain my self-respect?

Lord, nothing less than the hand that planted
  a thousand forests and poured the seven seas
  can impart to our hearts the impulse
  to love the unloved, the unloving, and the unlovely—
  a power beyond limits and foreign to reason.

Except, O Lord, we are convinced you love us,
   will love us down through the ages to come,
   until the seas become deserts and the forests
   are no more.
Outlasting any bond will be the everlasting covenant
   of life, somewhere keeping as one
        the family of God.
Keep before our vision the victory over the death
   and the resurrection of Jesus, an event
   to be lived, and relived, O God,
     where friends and enemies meet
      where the alienated come together
       when those outside are drawn in
         and those who dislike themselves are invited back
          and people like us,
            bound with the cords of resentment
              may rendezvous, and find at the old cross
            liberation at last.

May this be the week we inherit the earth,
   and when the whole Gospel of Christ
   is entrusted to us.
Then, while you keep telling us what we can do,
   we shall stop telling you what you cannot do.
Through Christ our risen Lord.

Amen.

THE POWER TO TALK BACK

Lord God, holy and ever to be worshipped,
glorious in name and reputation
    among all the people of the earth,
we ask you now,
teach us to pray,
for in learning how to pray,
we are learning how to live.

Walk with us into Paul's assertion that
  we be more than conquerors through Him who loved us.
We pray to be even more than conquerors
  through the impish defiance of humor,
  the gift to smile
at the terribly serious business around us,
the oblivious plodding of the folk for whom
each hour is so momentous and
each day a potential Armageddon.

To smile, yes, O God, and to be confident.
We ask to feel, think, and talk assertively.
You blessed the meek and said
  they would inherit the earth.
We have been blessing doormats instead,
the whining victims among us,
    as if being stepped on by an endless succession
    of people were a distinctively Christian privilege.
Lift us to our feet. Whisper in our ears.
Nudge us a bit to tell the world who our God is,
who we are,
and where we are coming from.

Help us, God almighty and ever-glorious King,
to talk back to our controlling spouses,
talk back to our children when they blackmail us,
talk back to the Pharisees in this church
   who recite our sins for our benefit,
talk back to the businesses run blindly by policy
   instead of thoughtfully by principle,
talk back to the friend who has all the answers
   to our problems,
talk back to a neighbor who would rather threaten
   than compromise,
talk back to those professionals who would prefer
   to intimidate than communicate,
talk back to the politicians who are deaf
   until election, and
meaning no disrespect, Lord,
in the face of indescribable adversity and
   humiliating pain, to have the privilege
   of talking back to you.
When they crucified Christ they did not know
   what they had done,
   but they do now,
   and it seems to us, O God,
   one crucifixion should be enough.
We could accomplish more, and with dignity
   in the name of Him who said,
"All power in heaven and earth has been given to me,"
   if we changed our vain suffering
   into useful anger.
In Jesus' name, Amen.

God Help Us!

Lord, we confess that as perfectionists
we do not have too many sins with which to bother you.
We are Bible-believing evangelicals
and that eliminates many mistakes right there.
We generally disagree with the Democratic party
because we know what they stand for.
We hedge on our income tax
because we disagree with the government and
we tend to think of women as subservient,
but the Bible is not too clear about that.
We support what our nation does militarily—
very close to what our enemies do,
but our motives are purer.
We have little time and money
to care for the poor and homeless
because we are very busy in Church.
We don't visit the sick in the hospitals,
but we inform the Pastors,
and we don't evangelize our city for Christ the Lord
because in church we want quality, not numbers.
We don't love you with our whole mind and soul
and strength, but we don't know of anyone else
who does either.
But we are deeply conscious
of our little compromises, Lord
because, as children of grace,
we tend to think of ourselves as outside the law.

Lord, let the scales drop from our eyes.
Amen.

GOD IS STILL LAUGHING

O God, we celebrate this day the victory of resurrection,
   your defiance of life over death.
Grant us, in the light of this victory,
   a deep and ongoing sense of humor.
If you ever wish, O Lord to see a group
   of over-grieving, over-sensitive, over-anxious,
   over self-conscious people, look at us.
How did this come to be, Lord?
What is the matter?
Grant us the transcendence of humor to see
   beyond the frustrations of this moment.
Grant us the recreation of humor, like Jesus,
   to play with children, sing, exchange stories,
   chat with friends, go to parties,
   and talk to the flowers.
Grants us the gentle arrogance of humor which
   holds graveside parties, laughs at cheap temptations,
   and tells the devil that if he didn't lie so much
   he'd be hilarious.
Grant us the reprieve of humor which insists that
   the potential destruction of the world by war some day
   ought not to rob us of a good laugh right now.
Help us, eternal Sovereign, to join with you
   in giggling with children, joking with the comics,
   and telling long and entertaining stories.
And, as Robert Frost prayed, "O Lord, if you will forgive
   our little jokes on you,
   we will forgive your great big joke on us."
If I am sorrowful, I shall wait for the irony
   of the Spirit when the appearance of doom
   turns to the reality of joy.
   There's always a joke, Lord,
   be patient 'till I get it.
Meanwhile, smile on us. Amen.

A Releasing Prayer

Our Creator God, for whom the whole earth was
   a week's production,
      who tests the creatures' might to brave the storm
   and who cherishes freedom more than security,
      we pray for the bittersweet courage to let go.

You gave the tiny bird wing-power to soar
   above the storm, and
You trust the great whales to return home through
   unmarked seas of terror and mystery.
Your love is your passion to see all things
   come into their own
through all your attributes of justice and mercy.

In our troubles you urge us to borrow miracles of wisdom
   to find our significance, and do it.
We, on the other hand, grasp tightly.
We are unable to let go.
We are dedicated to holding on to our children.
We insist that they need us now as they did back then.
We hold on to our loved ones who have said, "good-bye."
We hold on tightly to our routine, our prejudice,
      our possessions, our rituals, and the good looks
      we thought we once had.

The one "letting go" we know
in order to retain our youth is the metamorphosis
of changing fashions.
    We spend hours recapturing a lost dream
        and in repossessing a lost glory.

This moment, Lord, open these hearts
and hands of ours in a daring bid for freedom.

As a bird flutters its wings
        and squirms out from a tight fist,
            so may we open our hands to heaven.
Slowly we release some people we vainly sought to hold.
Slowly, we discover the heady power
of letting go of what we thought belonged to us.
Let them fly away until our generosity,
        our trust in you,
                and our capacity to love,
                        are all reborn.
Father, we are open to the grief of saying Good-bye.
            We have held on too, too long.
    We pray that your Spirit shall comfort us.
        We know you have released us, not abandoned us.
            Receive our adoration for letting us go—
                for being there when we need you—
                    for answering when we call you.
                        Through Christ our Lord.

Shalom!

A Prayer Leaving the Manger

All-powerful Conductor of the celestial symphony,
we learn more about you at the birth of Jesus
than at the birth and death of worlds
    like ours.
It is only the sight of new life, and the experience of
new hope which enable us to believe that
humiliation and adversity have their victories
but tomorrow
    is a new day.
In a time of boredom and emptiness
    replay the charm of Christmas.
In our hum-drum space
televise some talented chorus on a cosmic screen
    singing Glory to God in the Highest, or
    How Great Thou Art, or The Hallelujah Chorus,
    or When the Saints Come Marching In, or
    any lively favorite.
And let the good times roll until fears shrink
and confidence breaks loose—
    —and we discover your liveliness
not only in babies born in stables,
but in routine duties
and ordinary people.
Lead us back home with the Shepherds, O Lord,
who believe that on the darkest night
God is working, and
back home with the wise men who followed a star
to find their destiny
and were not disappointed.

Give us a Christmas present
    of powerful, enduring faith
so that we do not merely wait for miracles,
    but help do them.
For there are those who are sick, defeated,
    discouraged, ready to give up,
who do not recognize sly miracles in common places,
and who need the eyes of children once more
to see your charm everywhere.

    Lord, it is true! We are deluged with miracles—
miracles of healing, and beauty, and hope—
    —miracles of birth,
        of self-discovery,
            and forgiveness,
                miracles when the old become young
        and the young become mature—
                        MIRACLES all
                            everywhere.

Illumine us with Christmas radiance
    that we may be led from holidays to these holy days,
and that Christ, rejected by His nation,
    may find in us
His grateful and faithful family.

            In His name, Amen.

ADVENT PRAYER

Lord God, may Christmas come early this year
    to our family, our relatives cared for
    well in so many ways,
especially in the shopping we enjoy on Saturday
    and complain of on Sunday.
We are thinking of our adopted family,
    those to whom we were sent with the words:
    feed them, visit, heal, tell, baptize, love, witness,
    and give a cup of water.

Come early this year, Lord Jesus Christ,
find the people who have fallen in the cracks and
    are wrapped in the City's shadow;
for Lord, our icy indifference is probably the reason
    we don't see either you or them.
Lord God, hallways and parks are their bedrooms,
the crowded pavements are where they live and die,
and they eat the scraps from our bountiful tables.

Lord, come early this year
    for it is cold and crowded and everyone is busy.
Come early and surprise the ones who don't expect you.
Come early for the sake of the very young
    and the very old, the dying ones
    and the hopeless ones.
You have always been unashamed to be
    with them in the marketplace and city streets;
so prompt us who already know our lines,
    what to say and do, where to go and what to give,
    how to share generously and live gracefully,
so that this year we meet you often
and discover joy in different ways and places.
In His name. Amen.

CHRISTMAS

God of light and all comfort,
we, the human family, gather around you
for our celebration of Noel.
In a world of cynicism, despair, and terrible fear
of famine, war, and death,
the light of heaven shines again,
and the words ring from pole to pole, "Fear not."
We have you to thank for the children's laughter,
the sounds of singing,
the mighty anthems of high praise, the gifts which say,
"I love you,"
the warm embrace of family again,
and the glorious senses that here
in a corner of the vast universe
we are not alone.
It is, it will always be Christmas with you, Lord Jesus.
As bad as life can be
there will always be singing, and prayer,
and the words ringing, "Fear not."
There will always be the surprise of joy
when we have waited.
Those who feel left out and wandering in the dark night
will have a *kinship* with you.
And if not this moment, when night seems forever,
the dawn *will* come *triumphantly* and it will be
Christmas once more.
Thank you for your gift of yourself.
Should they stop us on the street and ask us
why we are happier than the rest, we will answer,
"Because Jesus Christ the Saviour is born, and
Christmas will *always* be."   Amen.

A Prayer for Ringing True

Lord God, who created all that we know of,
and what we shall learn of,
and all the truth of worlds we shall never know of—
who ignites the candles of heaven
and calls them suns—
all are an effulgence of your glory.
All are tiny lights of your brilliance
veiled by our mortality.
Halleluja, our Sovereign.

Shine openly in our living.
Joy is compromised by the lie of small sins,
and our light is stifled by fleeting shadows.
We have bargained the store away
in our clever negotiations with the devil
and we are amused to know
how much we can get away with.
As you have commanded light to shine out of darkness,
flood our hearts with this light.
In our marriages and friendships,
strike a blow for honesty in all things.
In doing business with children,
banish the destructive deceit,
this baby talk, these unkept promises,
and no-so-subtle coercions—
and inaugurate truthfulness.

May thy truth set the children free, O Lord.
Enable us to listen, to read, to learn,
to look in judgment's mirror so that
we can be at peace with what we tell ourselves.
May our business competitors agree that we are genuine,
and the marketplace gossip be
that we are so honest it is painful.
When we are inspected publicly for tell-tale signs
of our loyalty to the Lord Jesus Christ,
may we ring true like the singing of clear crystal.
Impart the Spirit's boldness so that we think sharply,
feel vividly, in our conversation speak reliably,
so that they say:
"They are authentic; their lives are an open book;
their word is pure gold."
Among a world of little people, O Lord God,
we pray to be giants—
trusted and unafraid.
Our Creator, in all that we are, now and always—
Help us to ring true!

A Child's Prayer

O God who has made the word Father
a magnificent title
and who is father and mother to us
whom He forgets not, no not for a moment,
nor where we are, and
what is on our hearts.
Taking wing in the turbulence of life,
we must gently settle on you
for a steady pace.
This, O God, as every year,
is the year of the children.
Our spirits are at home among the little ones,
with their joy thrown about,
and their funny songs,
and their wide-open eyes to catch it all.
How well we remember their prayers.

"God bless Mom, and Dad,
and bless our teachers,
and mean Joe who likes to pick on me,
and bless Mrs. Jones who hurts so bad in the hospital
at least that's what mom says . . .
and bless the president of our country and make sure,
please, that there are no more wars because . . .
well *you* know why,
in Jesus name. Amen . . ."

And we have not prayed much differently over the years,
perhaps more wisely
but not more sincerely or with greater faith.
Keep the child within us full of life and sight,
funny songs, energy, curiousity, trusting, friendly,
wanting to be surprised, faithful to some spoiled pet,
and up for a dare, day or night.

Forgive us for our little mischief
and some of our sinful fantasy.
Grant us time to play, to visit or write to Mrs. Jones,
to invest our imagination in the Holy Bible,
and to make goodness a refreshing delight
and not a long-face duty the adults make it.
Thank you for helping us learn happiness.
You are always sharing our burdens,
so when we laugh and play, will you not join us,
O God of beauty, O Spirit of Joy.

Through Jesus Christ, the Lord.   Amen.

A Prayer in Grief

God of mercy and Lord of comfort,
the one presiding judge in this and every world,
and the Sovereign who pours out His grace
in a springtime shower of freshness,
receive our gratitude that here it is morning
and we are still alive.
We are delighted with the knowledge that we celebrate
the resurrection
and that one morning we shall awake
knowing there will be no dark night awaiting us.
Embrace those here this morning who grieve over loss,
whatever it may be.
For those who have lost a person—but only for awhile,
or health, or a place, or a hope—but only for awhile,
whisper again a word from Jesus
that will heal and encourage as nothing else can.
For those who have lost an illusion,
a distant dream,
a marriage,
a youth,
even a gamble,
a forever,
reach down and kiss those for whom new beginnings
come slowly.

And when we are low,
forgive our games—our testing of you,
our rash promises to you, and our Pharisaism—
we point out and catalogue the sins of others
while they are doing the same to us—
small comfort, Lord Jesus, to a people
that had to be bathed in amazing grace from head to toe
before they could be forgiven—
before *we* could be redeemed
and adopted into your family.

In a day of trouble, O God,
place underneath us the everlasting arms
that we who should have learned a few things in life
may befriend others in their troubles.

In the name of Christ Jesus we pray.

Amen.

BAPTISM IN THE FAMILY

Our Father, now we have baptized these young persons
in your Name and we send them into the world.
They have felt our hands upon them,
and in this sacred moment may they now feel yours.

They have no idea what this baptism
will cost them over a lifetime,
but they will.

When the pressures of living lead them
to the threshold of evil, may they whisper,
"But I have been baptized."

When they are tempted to hide their light
under a bushel, may they remember,
"But I am baptized."

And at the conclusion of our way,
when the dusk leads into the darkness,
may they give thanks to you that
this seal of your fatherly benediction
was as indelible as your love.

We rejoice.
These disciples will always know who they are.

This very morning they are baptized!
Yes, in the name of the Father, and of the son,
and of the Holy Spirit.
Amen.

"HAPPY NEW YEAR!"

God of this and every world, of this and every time,
we smile with deep satisfaction at the beginning of the year,
that the Lord Jesus Christ wipes the slate clean.

We bid adieu, Our Lord, not solely to our folly,
  but to the memories which sear and burn in solitude.
We bid good-bye to dear companions
  we shall not see until the graduation.
We take snapshots of lost gambles,
  misguided ventures, and dashed hopes
  as we place them on the altar to be burned
  as an offering to the God of the second chance.
And more.

We who have faced disillusionment and defeat
  pray for grace to walk directly into
  a brand new start, comforted without certainty,
  clear headed without guidance,
  courageous but without direction, humming only
  "blessed assurance, Jesus is mine."
Then, when we least expect it, Lord, by great sign
  or gentle whisper, send a resurrection,
  the opening sentence for the next chapter.

So we honor and praise you, O God,
  not merely for the next chance,
  or the new beginning,
  but the new life.
We pray through Christ
  our crucified and risen Lord. Amen.

PRAYER BY RESPECTABLE PEOPLE

O Sovereign God,
Who holds the nations in the palm of His hand
and the one to whom all history points,
we confess to you that in the drama of our time
and perhaps the last time, we are without principles.

We hold the most profound convictions
    for insignificant matters and lack any deep value
    for the significant issues of our time.
Outside of our stalwart opposition to the end of
    civilization by war, we have collected
    the opinions of popular trends,
    community prejudice,
    and the pale tenets of middle-class respectability.
We know, O Lord, that our foreparents
    were burned at the stake for their beliefs,
    while we can't even get a decent argument going
    over ours.
At a time when people cry out for direction,
    we can only quote something
    without the personal meaning that convinces and
    points the way.
Forgive us for our preoccupation
    with our own immunity from minor embarrassments
    while people around us might do more
    with the salvation of our Lord Jesus Christ
    if they could see it made a radical difference in us.

Raise our eyes and hearts to where the people have
    great needs, so that we shall learn
    to rely on a God great enough to meet them.
Through Christ our Lord, have mercy.   Amen.

No Further Justification

There is no shortage of God's energy, *no* shortage.
   There is infinite power to bloom, to radiate,
    to care, to create, to speak, to take in,
    to see, to hear—
 in other words
    to live
       humanly.
And this living is itself
    the answer to death. It needs nothing
    beyond itself to be justified
    in the face of death.
We are, in fact, little gods who participate in God,
    or in idolatry; our lives exulting in the life,
    the other existence staving off death.
One becomes tired of living, not because
    there is a limit to God's energy,
    but because we people tend to measure
    God's power by our last mistake,
    His love by our last taste of futility,
    His bounty by our last fit of despair,
His grace seems never to finally blot out
    our memory of betrayal, and so it is only
    in viewing every dawn
    as evidence
that we are daily born again by faith
    in Jesus Christ
    that life
   and love
    become
     one.

              Amen.

Robert James St. Clair

is currently the Executive
Director of the Bay Area
Pastoral Counseling Center,
which he founded in 1976.
Formerly known as the Center
for Experiential Theology, the
center was incorporated in
1983 and is internationally
accredited as a service center
by the American Association
of Pastoral Counselors, with a
staff of five persons working in
four locations.

Ordained in the Presbyterian Church in 1951, Dr. St. Clair has
served churches in Cincinnati, Cleveland, and Akron; and is
currently Parish Associate Minister at the First Presbyterian
Church of Berkeley.

Dr. St. Clair is a graduate of Brooklyn College (A.B.), Biblical
Seminary in New York (S.T.B.), University of Cincinnati (M.A.),
Perkins School of Theology, Southern Methodist University
(S.T.M.), and Chicago Theological Seminary (Rel.D.). He was
Professor of Pastoral Theology in the Hamma School of
Theology, Wittenberg University (Springfield, Ohio) in 1968-75.
He teaches from time to time at the Pacific School of Religion
and serves as an adjunct professor in other schools within the
Graduate Theological Union (Berkeley, California).

Other books written by Dr. St. Clair include: *Neurotics in the
Church* (Revell, 1963); *The Adventure of Being You* (Revell,
1967); and *Faith Sharing Evangelism*, written with Dr. Richard
Moore (Presbyterian Church, U.S.A., 1985).

Titles Available from BIBAL Press:

Ivan J. Ball, Jr., *A Rhetorical Study of Zephaniah* [$16.95]

Duane L. Christensen, ed., *Experiencing the Exodus* [$7.95]

Norbert F. Lohfink, S.J., *Option for the Poor:*
    The Basic Principle of Liberation Theology in the Light of the Bible [$6.95]

A. Dean McKenzie, *Sacred Images and the Millennium:*
    Christianity and Russia (A.D. 988-1988) [$7.50]

Jo Milgrom, *The Binding of Isaac:*
    The Akedah -- A Primary Symbol in Jewish Thought and Art [$16.95]

William R. Scott, *A Simplified Guide to BHS (Biblia Hebraica Stuttgartensia)* [$5.95]

Robert J. St. Clair, *Prayers for People Like Me* [$6.95]

M. L. Baker & R. K. Songer, *Seven-Color Greek Verb Chart* [$2.95]

* * * * *

BIBAL Monograph Series

1   *Jesus Christ According to Paul:*
    The Christologies of Paul's Undisputed Epistles and the Christology of Paul
    Scott Gambrill Sinclair [$12.95]

2   *Enoch and Daniel:*
    A Form Critical and Sociological Study of Historical Apocalypses
    Stephen Breck Reid [$12.95]

3   *Prophecy and War in Ancient Israel:*
    Studies in the Oracles Against the Nations in Old Testament Prophecy
    Duane L. Christensen [$14.95]

* * * * *

Mail check or money order to: BIBAL Press
                                     P.O. Box 11123
                                     Berkeley, CA 94701   415/799-9252

Postage & handling ($1.00 per book, max. $3.00)
6.5% Sales Tax (California residents only)   May 1989

[*Please Note*: Prices subject to change without notice]